Stamped

poems by

Emma Alford

Finishing Line Press
Georgetown, Kentucky

Stamped

ACKNOWLEDGMENTS

Funmas—published in 2011 *Confidante Literary Magazine*
Double Life—published in 2011 *Confidante Literary Magazine*
411 Days—published in 2012 *Confidante Literary Magazine*

Postcard image for "Funmas" card name/ reference courtesy of Image
Source, Copyright James Hearne

Editor: Christen Kincaid

Cover Art: Cyle Barnes

Author Photo: Cain Barnes

Cover Design: Andy Howell

Printed in the USA on acid-free paper.
Order online: www.finishinglinepress.com
Also available on www.Amazon.com

Author inquiries and mail orders:
Finishing Line Press
P. O. Box 1626
Georgetown, Kentucky 40324
U. S. A.

Table of Contents

Correspondence

Cacophony

For Moose, my best friend

Correspondence

Everything's
BIGGER
in
TEXAS

SAN ANTONIO

EVERYTHING'S BIGGER IN TEXAS!
Photos © Richard Stockton
Digital Imaging © Terrell Creative

17 FEB

Hey Buddy!
I just thought that I would
send you a slice of
TEXAS!! You should
put this on your mirror.
I love you!
        -Cassidy
P.S. Cow Actual size

Emma Alford

DO NOT WRITE BELOW THIS LINE

0 86598 63133 8

Postmarked February 17, 2007

The first card I received
It felt strange; your address was always two numbers off,
one door down, to the right of mine.
I didn't know to expect mail from 641 miles away.
You never had to ask for my address, birthday, or shoe size.
And you were the only one who knew why I hate bar soap.

You'd only been gone a few weeks when you sent it out.
You told me to put it on my mirror, I did.
It fell down constantly, annoyed, I'd tape it back up each time.
I took it down to write this.

Another answer to this postcard from another time.
A joke about the size of the cow on the front,
how it was really that big, I still hear your sarcasm.
I remember the first time I visited. You convinced me that
Jackalopes were real, "They're native to Texas."
High and smiling, later that night you confessed your lie.

Emma!

-These are the cheap cards
everyone is getting ☺ If you
haven't already realized, there
is more stuff in the front
pocket of the purse. Hope
you like it. I was thinking...
Once this whole christian
thing blows over, I think we
should propose it be changed
to Funmas... Your thoughts?
I love you!

                    -Cassidy

Hope your Holidays
are the best!

Funmas

Last Christmas you sent the standard present package,
I had come to expect it every year.
A few weeks later you visited me while it was still cold.
It was the last time I saw you, but it doesn't feel like it.
It never seemed like we were very far from one another;
We never grew apart.
I still feel you now.
Something always kept us calling, mailing cards,
sending packages, buying plane tickets, and driving miles.
You're the only friend I ever bothered to buy Christmas gifts for.
We joked that our other friends were cheap.
This year I don't think I can stand buying one less gift

You were always the easiest to buy for, the first off my list.
So I think I'll mail something to your family.
Some old photos of us, A zine we made in junior high,
maybe a nice scented candle or ornate box.
Your mom loves decorative boxes, we laughed about this.
The last one I saw her with was filled with bits of you.
This exchange won't feel the same,
but I won't feel as much like I've lost something.
Last week I took your card to a tattoo shop in Nashville.
I had your sloppy boyish handwriting inked into my skin forever.
You would call me a hypocrite; I always hated the way you wrote.
Now it's something else, tragically beautiful, your epitaph.

Everything's **BIGGER** in **TEXAS**

EVERYTHING'S BIGGER IN NORTH TEXAS
Photos © Dennis Hallinan/FPG & Max Hunn/FPG

17 NOV 2008

LET US DARE TO
THINK, SPEAK
John Adams, 1765

USA FIRST-CLASS FOREVER

Yo Emma!
    Your mail box isn't
hungry today! This post
Card represents the
mind set of everyone
here. (kill me) We need
to get together soon
and get shitty. I love you
                    —Cassidy

© Distributed by Smith-Southwestern, Inc. • Printed in Singapore
www.smith-southwestern.com • 1195068

Emma Alford

0 86598 63167 3

Double life

We were starting college when you sent this postcard.
I think you were fed up with cowboys.
Your school had a rodeo, not football, team.
And this was after I called and you answered
"I'm in a cop car, so I may need to call you back"
It was weird to hear you complain about anything.
You always told me I was too quick to hate,
you were just so quick to love—and I think
you had too much of it in a world that wouldn't understand it.

You said, "kill me," the two lighthearted words seize in my chest now.
When we were younger, we wrote our last wishes out
on tiny sheets of paper,
exchanged and swore in jest to carry them out
should anything happen.
Were we setting ourselves up for this all those years ago?
I found the tiny folded piece of paper, I followed it faithfully.
We had sunflowers and Weezer, and I didn't wear all black.
Your sister and I gave your eulogy, the hardest words I ever spoke,
the difference in my verb tense choking me.

I vowed to live a double life. I will love what you loved,
destroy what you feared and complete what you started.
I'll get us to New Zealand and I'll stop smoking cigarettes.
Taking the fire from your life and putting it to mine.
I can't condense you, I can't feel you, in five minutes of words.
But maybe I can in a lifetime of actions. I promise
I'll always carry you around my neck, tucked into my chest.

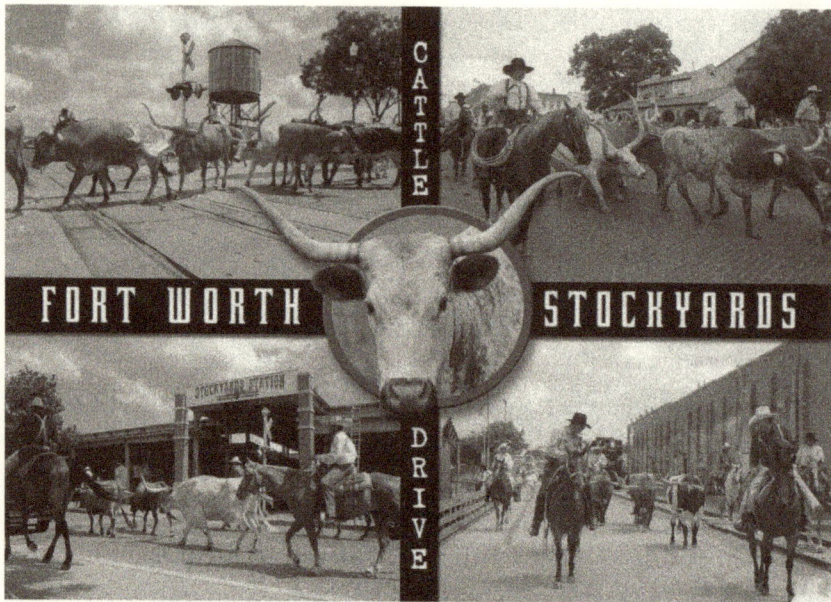

FORT WORTH STOCKYARDS
Cattle Drive

One of Fort Worth's greatest treasures, the annual cattle drive pays homage to Fort Worth's roots and the cattle industry that put this city on the map.

Photos by Steve Gibson/Tony Marinella © Terrell Creative

LAME

Emma!   see you in 2
               weeks

Emma Alford

-After looking at
this post card Mississippi
looks pretty good.
Here's some mail
So people know you
got peeps in other places
                    -Cassidy

yo! I'm getting
the work out!

DO NOT WRITE BELOW THIS LINE

0 86598 67150 1

Planetary Love

There was a time I thought I was in love with you;
I heard you singing Van Morrison while
you thought I was sleeping.
It was a planetary love, natural but calculated, inevitable.
We needed each other to revolve around but
all those years our universe was expanding; it was something we
couldn't know or expect and you fell out of orbit.
I collapsed in on myself—left to atrophy now

You wrote this postcard, two weeks before you'd visit.
Our last conversation, two weeks before I was to see you.
I delivered some news about an acquaintance of ours dying,
we both acted more upset than we truthfully were and you asked,
"How come every time we talk there is always bad news?"

We made the planned trip, driving to the place you last existed,
burning up the roads
that brought me to you, that took you from me.
Slept in the last bed you did, showered with your shampoo.
I could feel you there, you were still so tangible.
Casual conversations danced around the notion that you were dead.

In a high school play,
we took the roles of 100-year-old best friends
Our estimation was that our characters seemed pretty accurate.
Years from then, when everyone we cared for had left us
or died, we'd share a couch reminiscing together.

I can't see that far ahead anymore;
I am paralyzed in that past without a future.
We thought we could own the world then,
screaming our punk anthems
at the top of our lungs, "This life is what you make it."

TX-S-104 TEXAS
6168

Printed in Florida
Made in U.S.A.

Dist by JAS. (972) 442-1209

© beachhut@bellsouth.net
Beach Hut. Inc. 407-299-0225

Emma—
HAPPY Really Early Birthday!!
— I know the gifts are really random
but only when I have money do gifts
compliment each other. Each item
seemed good to party with.
Nothing says party like bendable
aliens! I hope you can come visit
me soon. It will be cooler this time!!
I Love You! Hooray for 19! (Lame)
—Cassidy

You Are the Compliment

It says hooray,
Happy early birthday!
Really random aliens to each other
this time, only I party.
I do have money but gifts seemed lame
Each item nothing, bendable
For cooler gifts…
Can you come visit me soon? When?
I really hope—know I will be good.
Cassidy, party like 19.

With love, Emma

*This poem is an anagram of the corresponding postcard.

Cacophony

Our Shadows like Giants

You brightened the sky—
The wheels
On the pavement
My world turned upside down
And right back up—
again   again

        As you fell down and met the ground

          A seatbelt tightened

          A radio blared

        But the glass was louder

Watching a grainy grey asphalt
Turn darker
As the dirt and grit loosened
With a sigh   she closed her eyes

      illuminating

Your scene
Our shadows
Like giants

On Praying

Glancing at my phone at a quarter past two in the morning, four missed calls from a number I don't often see. I return the call and the voice seems worried but calm and eerily reassuring, so I find comfort in sleep for a few hours. Another call drops my stomach and I drop too. I felt so compelled to this thing, such a foreign idea for myself, a prayer. I ordered myself and my thoughts, disregarded my lack of faith and begged for one thing, the only thing I'd ever asked for. I did this for five days with passion. I spoke them out loud and watched all my big pleading prayers turn to tiny fizzing whims as they floated from my lips. They couldn't reach her. The strangest day of my life was standing in the church I grew up in while my faithful grandfather read his holy scriptures and my faithless mouth gave her eulogy. I left feeling more angry and empty than before, turning one thought over in my head: faith is futile.

Us

Like birds we migrate through the spaces of life
It must be understood that a visit is made under
no obligations but love and need.
Our feathers change and fade where we stand.
When healthy, we retain the ability to re-grow the ones
we have lost, our coats shine again.

We are bound to life's endless skies always searching,
moving distances towards some home, a place to visit.
We fly faster through billowing winds and slow down rarely.
We depend upon one another for direction.
The idea of a single-self living
wholly alone is frightening and foreign.

We take easy breaths, spread our wings and disown loneliness;
We are evermore able. A self is forlorn and lost,
but for this idea: a letter
can be set in place of a visit. The distances we cannot fly can
be covered by inked words on paper.
Such a novelty conjoining two selves.

A self to send and a self to receive
this action of love-- abolishing loneliness and
forging a bond that is Us. But birds can't write postcards,
their talons can't be tamed. And neither
can I. My fingers are broken, directionless
Pen to paper impossible, this distance impassable.

Transplantation

I could never understand what's worse:
The sound of someone dying
Or the sound of someone keeping them alive.
What's left when a person goes?
I hope you didn't know you were dying;
I can only believe that every part of you was fighting.
If I hadn't met your eyes
Memories and feelings aside
I wouldn't know enough to surmise
If they'd wear them better than you all those years of our lives.

I never could tell if your heart beat faster in their chest
Than it did in yours before
They pulled it from your lifeless breast
Never to know if all they tore
From your within was fit to work.
Through your life, to the very last end
You chose to mend.
Now I'm left to wonder how much of you lingers
In those tissues and fibers and all that stayed.
Cassidy, all of you will never fade.

Burn Marks

We smoked cigarettes in the clumsiest way,
burning holes in the roofs of cars on the way to school
or on gravel roads.

We hid our pot from parents in shiny tins
that once held cough drops.
We wore these fitted tees with piffy remarks
stretched over our small chests,
boasting more confidence than we ever felt.

We clutched at invincibility together, filled diaries and talked plans.

We cut our hair senior year and
got tattoos with stretched meanings,
because we were just 18.
We wore dresses that made our legs look longer
and we talked about college or novels about it anyway.

There is a grain bin road a mile outside our town,
close to my sister's old house,
where we would park and wait out the last minutes before curfew.

Clinging to these moments and conversations and your bandanas
This nostalgia is nauseating and tranquilizing
If I could, I'd burn a 1000 holes in your roof.

411 Days

411 days since
She doesn't frequent my dreams now,
no longer my first waking thought
but over coffee
or after a shower
a Van Morrison song
She floods into me.

A box of photos sits on a desk I avoid.
To open it means it's over, she's over.
She still exists in these spaces
I can't visit.
A grain bin road.
The house next door.
The entire city of New York.

I have gridlocked myself in my own life
Preventing the inevitable from happening.

The best feelings had are behind me
Encapsulated by her.
The necklace of her
is never cold on my neck
I sleep in her now
hoping for some return, if only in dreams.

V- Neck

Last week I was grappling with the loss of her t-shirt
The soft blue cotton v-neck, hole punched from too many washes
Had accidently been thrown in the wastebasket
Like a rag used to dust off our bookcases

I hadn't worn it in a year
Yet I held onto it because it once held her
It had been a perfect fit
Draping over both her narrow shoulders

I am told—it is unbecoming to continue to grieve so thoroughly
Unamerican or unchristian—unnatural or unhealthy
So I breathe and I rub soap between my wistful hands constantly
I have read—everything we ever let go of has claw marks

Holding Ash

"Human Remains" is such a cold, ambiguous phrase
what remains after all, is dust and unbroken bit of bones and teeth
too strong against the funeral home's fires to burn
and I'm still unsure what's human about remains

Grasping for ashes is like reaching for the thinnest grains of sand
Your hand turns chalky white—
bits of bone get stuck beneath a fingernail
There is nothing to romanticize in this
Life so far from those granules slipping between shaking fingertips

I thought that I might find her,
3000 miles from any soil she'd ever graced
By placing her in the walls of an 800-year-old castle
Or sprinkling her in the river floating past the Eye

She wasn't there
Or in the teeth and nails caking my palms
Further away now than she ever was
Returning to dust as anything does

Emma Alford is a writer from the Mississippi Delta. She is an editor and contributor for *The East Nashvillian* magazine. She lives in Nashville, Tennessee with her over-loved, overweight orange tabby cat.